Play to Earn

The Advent of the Gaming Metaverse

Table of Contents

Chapter 1. Introduction

Welcome to a thrilling new era where gaming and wealth creation merge, reshaping the face of the digital world as we know it! In this Special Report, we journey into the exciting phenomenon of "Play to Earn: The Advent of the Gaming Metaverse." Our meticulously researched and comprehensible piece explores the fascinating intersections of video gaming, blockchain, and decentralized finance. Herein, we unravel how ordinary players can earn real-world income simply by traversing virtual landscapes. Regardless of your prior understanding, our report is crafted to enlighten novices and experts alike, uncovering the potentialities and novelties of this burgeoning ecosystem. Offering analysis, expert opinions, case studies, and forecasts, our Special Report delivers a comprehensive perspective of these revolutionary landscapes. Transform how you view your gaming escapades and dive into the future today! Order our Special Report to fully grasp how you can turn playtime into paytime.

Chapter 2. Setting the Stage: The Evolution of Gaming

In the not-so-distant past, gamers worldwide could scarcely dream of earning a living from their digital adventures. Yet, today, that dream is steadily becoming reality. Welcome to the era of 'Play to Earn,' a remarkable convergence of technological advancements, globalized economies, and ingenious human imagination. This unprecedented paradigm shift didn't materialize overnight. Its roots run deep into the storied history of video gaming itself, a fascinating journey of evolution and innovation worth exploring.

2.1. Before the Dawn: The Pioneering Years

The first video games emerged in the mid-20th century, a time of radical innovation in electronics and computing. In the 1950s and 60s, computers were predominantly the realm of academia and major corporations. Scientists and engineers coded the first rudimentary video games using archaic computer machinery, merely as demonstrations of computer programming prowess and not for public consumption.

It was not until the 1970s, with the advent of consumer electronics, that the age of commercial video gaming truly began. Companies like Atari and Magnavox produced the first generation of home gaming consoles. Games like Pong and Space Invaders took the world by storm, ushering in an age of public enthusiasm for video games.

2.2. From Pixels to Profits: The Rise of Commercial Gaming

The 1980s and 1990s brought forth an explosion of creativity and technological advancement within the gaming industry. Household names, such as Nintendo, Sega, and later Sony, established themselves as giants of the gaming world during this era, introducing iconic franchises like Super Mario, Sonic the Hedgehog, and Final Fantasy. More importantly, these two decades saw gaming transitioning from a niche hobby to a multi-billion dollar industry. The concept of 'playing for profit' debuted, albeit in a primitive form, as lucrative tournaments and professional gaming gained traction.

During this period, the seeds for 'play to earn' were sown in the form of player transactions. Role-Playing Games (RPGs) and Massively Multiplayer Online (MMOs), like Ultima Online and World of Warcraft, allowed players to sell rare in-game items for real-world currency, a controversial practice at the time. But, this established a vital precedent that virtual goods hold authentic value.

2.3. The Digital Renaissance: Online Gaming and Microtransactions

Advancements in the Internet and the widespread access to home computers in the 2000s led to a seismic shift in gaming: the rise of online multiplayer. Suddenly, players from across the globe were able to occupy shared virtual spaces, fostering an emerging trend - social gaming. This phenomenon nurtured a whole new marketplace for in-game purchases and microtransactions.

The launch of Farmville on Facebook in 2009 was a seminal moment in the monetization of gaming. As one of the first games to successfully implement a 'freemium' model, players could progress in the game for free but had the option to purchase digital goods to enhance their gaming experience. The game's success established the freemium model as a viable business strategy, paving the way for future free-to-play games with profitable in-game economies.

2.4. Unfurling the Blockchain: The Dawn of Decentralized Gaming

The remarkable advent of blockchain technology added a transformative layer to gaming's economic landscape. With blockchain enabling secure, transparent, and traceable transactions of digital assets, the infrastructure for a truly decentralized gaming economy came into focus.

In 2017, the launch of CryptoKitties took the gaming and blockchain world by storm, demonstrating the potential of Non-Fungible Tokens (NFTs) for representing unique digital assets. The game featured blockchain-backed digital cats, each unique and owned by the player. These digital pets were not merely leased from the game's developers but were actual properties that players could trade or sell. This paved the way for a truly 'Play to Earn' economy where players could accrue wealth from their activities in virtual landscapes.

In the years that followed, several 'Play to Earn' games emerged, combining gameplay with NFTs and cryptocurrency transactions. Axie Infinity, one of the most successful among them, has managed to build a vibrant ecosystem where players can earn serious income through their strategic gameplay and smart investments.

No perspective of gaming would be complete without acknowledging this dramatic shift in the potential of play. The advent of the 'Play to Earn' model marks a new epoch in the evolution of gaming—one where the boundaries between virtual and physical economies blend seamlessly. The gaming stage today sets a course for an exhilarating future, fueled by the revolutionary visions of developers, the passionate commitments of players, and the undeniably transformative power of technology.

Chapter 3. Unveiling the Concept: What is Play to Earn?

Understanding the realm of video gaming and its potential impact on wealth generation requires delving into the innovative concept of Play to Earn. This rapidly growing sector fuses traditional gaming techniques with avant-garde methodologies of financial reward, forming a bridge between entertainment and income generation.

3.1. The Evolution of Gaming

In its early stages, the gaming industry was solely about entertainment, where players would compete for high scores or personal satisfaction - no financial rewards were involved. The advent of online gaming in the late 1990s opened up new avenues for interaction, competition, and collaboration between players on a global scale. Freemium models were introduced, allowing users to play for free while offering in-game purchases to enhance their gaming experience.

However, these models led to an unprecedented power imbalance. High spending players dominated leaderboards while the majority lacked the financial means to compete effectively. This unfair dynamic provoked widespread dissatisfaction, instigating the search for a more equitable solution.

3.2. The Paradigm Shift: Play to Earn

The Play to Earn (P2E) model is an innovative solution to elements of inequity within the gaming ecosystem. Unlike traditional models where players spend money to participate or get ahead, P2E stipulates that players could be compensated for their time, effort, and skills within a game. Earnings can be in the form of cryptocurrencies, fungible tokens, non-fungible tokens (NFTs), or other digital assets that can often be converted into real-world value.

For the first time, the digital gaming world and tangible economic models intersected, giving rise to digital economies with their virtual goods and services. Gaming was no longer a money-sink – it was a potential income source, reshaping the perceived value of time spent in-game. Moreover, this promising model removes barriers for those financially less privileged, making competitiveness in the gaming space accessible to all.

3.3. The Underlying Technology: Blockchain

Fueling this revolutionary model are blockchain and decentralized finance (DeFi). Similar to how blockchain has disrupted other industries, it penetrates the gaming industry to foster new ways of generating and distributing wealth.

Blockchain guarantees transparency and security of all transactions made within a game. Its decentralized nature means no central authority can manipulate or control a player's assets. Every interaction is registered on a public ledger, providing an unmatched level of fairness and security.

3.4. Cryptographic Tokens in Gaming

A core component of the Play to Earn model is the use of cryptographic tokens. These tokens represent a player's earned value, which can then be traded or sold within or outside the game environment. There are two main types of tokens in P2E: fungible and non-fungible.

Fungible tokens are interchangeable, like digital currencies such as Ethereum or Bitcoin. In-game, these could be rewards for winning a tournament or completing certain tasks. Non-fungible tokens (NFTs), on the other hand, are unique and can't be replicated. NFTs can represent in-game assets, like characters, weapons, or power-ups. This attributes a certain degree of rarity to such digital assets, contributing significantly to their perceived worth.

3.5. Real-World Applications

Already, we are seeing the Play to Earn model being applied in successful gaming projects. An intriguing case is Axie Infinity, a game where players breed, raise, and battle fantasy creatures called Axies. Players can sell or trade their Axies or other in-game items for real-world profit on various marketplaces that accept crypto, making it rewarding for their time and effort invested in raising powerful creatures.

In conclusion, the 'Play to Earn' paradigm is transforming the gaming landscape by providing tangible rewards to players. This innovative model, underpinned by blockchain technology, is not only empowering gamers worldwide but also pioneering an entirely new digital economy. However, it's important to recognize that while the potential for profit exists, it's still crucial to understand the dynamics of the specific game, the volatile nature of cryptocurrencies, and the risks involved before diving into the P2E world.

As we embark further into the metaverse era, we can only anticipate that P2E will broaden to encompass more sophisticated digital economies. Truly, the Play to Earn rise is a seismic shift in the gaming world and represents a revolution in how we perceive value within digital realms.

Chapter 4. Cracking the Code: Blockchain and Gaming

Understanding the synergy of blockchain technology and gaming requires peering into the fundamental aspects of both domains. They represent two broad vertices of the modern digital era, each powerful in their own space.

4.1. Blockchain: The Trust Machine

Blockchain, often referred to as a "trust machine," serves as the bedrock of decentralized finance (DeFi) and has transformed various digital transactions. Its efficacy lies in decentralization, transparency, immutability, and security. With no central controlling entity, each participant (or node) in the blockchain network has equal control and access to the entire transaction history. Each transaction is verified by several nodes, thus eliminating the need for trust.

The inalterability of blockchain transactions ensures that once confirmed, it can't be reversed, providing a trail of verifiable and truthful transaction history. Thanks to its use of cryptography, security is paramount, with each transaction sealed and protected from third-party tampering.

4.2. Gaming: The Digital Escape

Video gaming, on the other hand, draws millions globally with its magnetic world of creativity and escapism. It offers players a platform to explore and arm-wrestle challenges, leaving them fascinated and glued to their devices. Video games create virtual economies where players can earn, trade, and lose in-game assets. These assets, however, have always been under the control of game developers.

4.3. Fusing Blockchain and Gaming: An Overview

The fusion of blockchain technology in gaming unveils a new paradigm. It offers a chance for players to take possession of their in-game assets and transform them into a source of real-world income. In effect, gaming is not just an avenue for pleasure but also a means to economic ends.

One remarkable facet brought about by blockchain technology in gaming is the tokenization of digital assets. Traditionally, any asset earned or created in the gaming world had no utility beyond that specific game environment. However, with the tokenization of these assets on a blockchain, they assume a value and existence outside the game.

Every collectible, property, and token in these games can be tokenized as NFTs (Non-Fungible Tokens), unique digital assets that are transferrable to other players, sold on marketplaces, or even used in other games. This transfer and trading of assets form a part of the decentralized finance model.

4.4. Case Study: Axie Infinity

To better understand the practical implementation, let's consider Axie Infinity, a Pokemon-inspired digital pet universe where players earn tokens by taking part in battles and quests. In Axie world, players can breed, earn, and trade Axies (the digital pets), all represented as NFTs on the Ethereum blockchain. More significantly, these tokens can also be sold on cryptocurrency exchanges for real money.

Since each player's investment and effort help add value to the Axie universe, it adopts a Play-to-Earn model. The more active and successful a player is within the game environment, the more tokens are earned, leading to potential financial gains.

4.5. The Future Outlook

As gaming and blockchain continue to merge, we are witnessing the creation of whole virtual economies. Extending beyond just games, the advent of Metaverses - vast, interactive virtual realities made up of countless digital universes - promises limitless potential for wealth creation and recreation. Similar to our physical world, these Metaverses would house virtual businesses, properties, and engaged communities, all backed by the authenticity and security of blockchain technology.

More blockchain-based games are following the Play-to-Earn model, providing increasing opportunities for gamers to generate income from their playtime. Developers are now considering gamers not merely as consumers but as stakeholders who can contribute to and profit from the game's ecosystem.

As we look ahead, the intertwining of gaming and blockchain heralds a future where digital economies aren't adjuncts of the gaming experience but intrinsic elements. Every action, interaction, purchase, or trade in the gaming environment will have tangible economic implications and opportunities in the real world.

Despite the budding state of this fusion, it's clear that blockchain's inherent capabilities could fill the systemic gaps in today's gaming industry, such as valueless in-game assets and a monopolistic distribution of wealth. Gaming could thus make blockchain more relatable and tangible, spiriting us into a revolutionary era of "Play to Earn."

However, for the greatest yield, this new field will require awareness, deep understanding, and strategic thinking. As more people become educated about the potential of a blockchain-based gaming metaverse, new opportunities will continuously emerge.

These cryptographically secure digital playgrounds are the starting point of an exhaustive revolution in how we perceive wealth, interact with digital assets, and even the nature of work and play.

With a robust blockchain network serving as the foundation, the digital gaming landscape is primed to be indomitable, radically transforming our perspectives of the gaming world and beyond.

Chapter 5. The Economic Shift: Traditional Gaming vs Play to Earn

As we transition into an increasingly digital world, the gaming industry has been at the forefront of these transformations. For decades, traditional video games have provided a rich source of entertainment for millions of users globally. These traditional games, often developed and marketed by large corporates, offered players an escape from reality into mesmerizing virtual worlds. The economic model here was simple: gamers bought the software or a subscription, and any in-game purchases translated into revenue for the game developers and publishers.

However, a new paradigm, "Play to Earn," fueled by blockchain technology and decentralized finance (DeFi), threatens to disrupt this conventional model.

5.1. The Traditional Gaming Economic Model

The traditional gaming economic model can be perceived as a one-way transaction. Gamers purchase access to the game, and in return, they obtain the right to participate in the game's narrative, missions, and quests. Often, microtransactions are employed, where gamers buy virtual goods, ranging from cosmetic enhancements for their avatars to advanced in-game tools or weapons that enhance their gameplay. However, the revenue generated, either through the initial purchase or via in-game transactions, remains profits accumulated by game developers.

For the player, scores, achievements, and progress are trapped within the confines of each specific game. The value created by the countless hours spent playing the game does not transcend beyond the gaming platform. Furthermore, if the game's servers were shut down, all the power-ups, virtual tools, and rewards accumulated by gamers would cease to exist.

5.2. The Play to Earn Economic Model

Play to Earn offers an exciting twist to this established norm. By utilizing blockchain technology, it transforms the economic model from one-way transactions to an ecosystem where the value flows both ways. Now, players are not just consumers but active participants in wealth creation. The gaming universe becomes more than just a gameplay arena; it evolves into a digital economy.

In a Play to Earn model, gamers can own in-game assets as Non-Fungible Tokens (NFTs), which are tokens with verified uniqueness and scarcity. These assets can be anything within the game, such as avatars, weapons, land, or creatures, which players can buy, sell, or trade on blockchain marketplaces. The real-world value of these assets gives players the potential to earn income by playing games.

Moreover, these games often have their native crypto tokens, which players can earn as rewards. Players can use these tokens within the game, or they can cash out by trading them on cryptocurrency exchanges.

Beyond this, strong player communities build other economic opportunities such as digital real estate, virtual goods and services businesses, or even create income by fulfilling tasks for other players within the game.

5.3. Case Study: Axie Infinity

Axie Infinity, a blockchain-based online game, is a prime example of Play to Earn's potential. Players can earn Smooth Love Potion (SLP), an in-game token that they can trade on cryptocurrency exchanges for other cryptocurrencies like Ethereum. They raise, battle, and trade Axies — adorable creatures that are NFTs on the Ethereum blockchain.

The game first gained traction in the Philippines, where some players could earn an income surpassing their local minimum wage, particularly during COVID-19's height when traditional job opportunities were scarce. The game's economic model presents an interesting case of how the lines between work and play can blur in the Virtual Economy.

5.4. The Shift in Economics

It's clear that Play to Earn transforms gaming from a mere recreational activity to becoming an active participant in wealth creation in the Digital Economy. They allow an inclusive financial system where anyone with an internet connection can participate and earn benefits.

However, like any paradigm shift, it comes with its sets of challenges. Regulatory concerns, especially about crypto-assets taxation, the stability of asset values, and user security, are pivotal issues that the system needs to tackle. We are in the early stages of a profound shift in digital economics, and as with the rise of any disruptive technology, its advantages and long-term impacts remain to be seen.

With blockchain's transparent and decentralized nature at its foundation, the Play to Earn model could prove to be not just an evolution in gaming but a revolution in digital economics. It's clear that the economic landscape within the gaming world is not what it used to be. As we forge into this new era of the gaming metaverse, it is truly an exciting time for both gamers and investors alike.

This shift indicates a future where the virtual world mirrors our reality more closely than ever before, blurring the lines between digital and physical, work and play, consumer and creator. Whether you're a gamer, investor, developer, or observer, understanding these economic shifts is paramount in navigating this new entrancing, confounding, and potentially lucrative universe that we're beginning to play, and earn, in.

Chapter 6. The Players and Pioneers: Key Figures in the Gaming Metaverse

The modern narrative of video gaming can't be written without acknowledging the players and pioneers who have blurred the lines between the virtual and the real, creating a revolutionizing platform for wealth creation. Blockchain technology intertwines with gaming, and a new model of 'play to earn' emerges from these depths, those who understand its workings, evolve with it, and harness its potential become heralds of this new digital era.

6.1. The Protagonists: Players Fueling the Gaming Economy

Perhaps the most important set of individuals in this new landscape are the players - the users who engage with these platforms, immersing themselves in the gaming world, carrying out tasks, missions, and objectives while progressively earning virtual currencies with real-world value. Players, erstwhile consumers of digital content, have morphed into valued contributors to the blockchain economy.

This shift from a consumption-based model to a contribution-based one has altered the gaming psychology. The players, once prospective buyers, are now active earners, often challenging the professional boundaries. Blockchain gaming platforms such as Axie Infinity, Crytovoxels, and Decentraland have gained significant traction by offering players opportunities to meet and exceed their physical-world income in virtual habitats.

6.2. Visionaries Behind the Screen: Game Developers

At the heart of these advancements reside the game developers who cleverly integrate gaming with blockchain technology. These unseen operators design the game mechanics, monetization structures and the systems of reward that lure players into these new gaming ecosystems. In 'play-to-earn' platforms, game developers create the blueprint that facilitates the storage, accumulation, and trade of in-game assets.

Whether it's the visionaries at Sky Mavis, the creators of Axie Infinity, or the developers behind Somnium Space, Cryptovoxels, and Decentraland, their work revolutionizes conventional gaming, transforming it into a productive and profitable endeavor.

6.3. The Crypto Sages: Decentralized Finance (DeFi) and Blockchain experts

Accompanying the gaming revolution are the decentralized finance (DeFi) and blockchain experts who provide the underlying structure for these 'play to earn' platforms. Decentralized finance allows the democratization of the gaming economy, by decentralizing the ownership of in-game assets.

These blockchain cryptographers and DeFi mavericks from foundations like Ethereum, Polygon, and Flow have given rise to non-fungible tokens (NFTs) and other unique digital assets that players can own, trade, or even lease, forging a thriving virtual economy.

6.4. New Merchants of the Metaverse: NFT Traders and Investors

Next in this dynamic ecosystem, discover the role of NFT traders and investors who drive the marketplace dynamics of the gaming metaverse. These virtual tycoons symbolize the shift towards a tokenized economy where digital assets possess real-world value.

The actions of NFT traders, their decisions, their investments, the virtual real estates they acquire, the digital artwork they commission, and the tokens they trade construct an intricate mesh of economic activity that's constantly shaping and reshaping the gaming environment.

6.5. The Story Weavers: Enthusiastic Community and Content Creators

Last and yet foremost, the gaming metaverse owes a debt of gratitude to the enthusiastic community of gamers and content creators who support this emerging landscape. Their passion for gaming, their creative endeavors to craft character skins or design virtual architectural wonders, their blog posts, videos, and their active participation in developing and upholding the game's lore, significantly contribute to the expansion of this ecosystem.

To conclude, the gaming metaverse will continue to see regular breakthroughs due to its organic and open-ended nature. As the range of potentialities open up, the characters of the gaming metaverse will continue to evolve. From average gamers turned digital entrepreneurs, to the visionaries building bountiful virtual realms, to the meticulous traders brokering pixelated assets, and the fervent fans weaving the fabric of the metaverse together - they all are the players and pioneers shaping the future of gaming.

Chapter 7. Decoding Decentralized Finance in Gaming

Decentralized Finance, commonly referred to as DeFi, is the intersection of cryptocurrency, blockchain technology, and financial services. It is a financial system built on public blockchains like Ethereum, BSC (Binance Smart Chain), and others. Traditional financial systems entirely rely on intermediaries such as banks, brokerages, or insurance services, whilst DeFi applications operate without the need for these intermediaries. DeFi advocates argue that this leads to a more efficient, open, and transparent financial system.

7.1. Understanding DeFi Basics

To get started, it's essential to understand how blockchain technology underlies DeFi. Blockchain is a type of database that collects information together in groups, or blocks. Each new piece of information that follows a newly added block is put together in a newly formed block that is added to the chain. When applied to the financial world, secure transactions can be made directly between two parties without the need of a trusted third-party, such as a bank or payment service.

Cryptocurrencies, which are digital or virtual forms of currency, are the means of trade in the blockchain cosmos. In gaming, these can be in forms of coins, gems, or any other token which enables economic interactions within the game.

Using smart contracts, protocols are written in lines of code and set up on the blockchain to automatically execute transactions when certain conditions are met. These self-executing contracts with the terms of the agreement directly written into lines of code exist across a decentralized blockchain network.

7.2. Impact of DeFi on Gaming Economy

Traditionally, the gaming industry had a centralized financial system, where the developers or platform providers held all the economic power. However, the advent of DeFi changed this monolithic structure. Decentralized finance in gaming transforms players into stakeholders. Players can now own assets and even earn real money, changing the dynamic between players and developers.

In the DeFi gaming world, in-game assets such as weapons, characters, land, or resources can be tokenized into cryptocurrencies. Players can trade these assets with others in the ecosystem or even sell them for real money. This gives rise to a new model: Play-to-Earn games.

The Play-to-Earn model allows gamers to make a living by playing games. Players can earn tokens by completing in-game achievements or tasks. These tokens can be exchanged for cryptocurrencies, which can be exchanged again for real-world currencies, bringing real economic return for virtual activities.

7.3. Notable DeFi Gaming Projects

One game representing the play-to-earn model via DeFi is Axie Infinity. Players can buy, breed, and trade digital pets (Axies) as NFTs (Non-Fungible Tokens). These NFTs can then be used in battles to win more tokens, or directly sold in the marketplace.

Decentraland, another noteworthy project, is a virtual world where players can buy land, build on it, and monetize their content. The land and assets are Ethereum-based tokens.

CryptoKitties, one of the first blockchain games, lets players breed, collect, and even sell one-of-a-kind creatures, each represented as a unique token on the Ethereum blockchain.

These games showcase the potential of DeFi in the gaming industry and its impact on the broader economy.

7.4. Challenges and Considerations

While DeFi presents a groundbreaking move for the gaming economy, it's not without its challenges. The main issues involve security risks, including smart contract bugs and hacks. Moreover, the DeFi world is still heavily unregulated, which can lead to potential scams and losses.

Also, it's worth noting the environmental considerations of cryptocurrencies and blockchain technology. These systems require significant computational power, which translates into high energy use. As a result, there have been increasing concerns about the environmental impact.

7.5. Future Prospects

Despite the challenges, DeFi in gaming holds impressive prospects. With the rise of NFTs and growing awareness of cryptocurrencies, we're likely to see more DeFi attributes in games. More gamers will pivot towards play-to-earn models, and with this shift, game development itself will transform to cater to these demands. Inclusivity, fairness, and transparency will become key concerns.

In conclusion, DeFi is reshaping the gaming economy, transforming players into stakeholders, and revolutionizing how we perceive value in gaming. As we continue to explore this realm, one thing is clear: The world of gaming is set for an exciting overhaul step by step, block by block.

Chapter 8. Case Studies: Success Stories in the Gaming Metaverse

The rise of the "Play to Earn" phenomenon has redefined how we perceive gaming as a purely leisure activity. It has fostered a unique gaming economy that allows players to earn real-world value while enjoying the thrill of virtual adventures. Numerous success stories have been documented, spotlighting the vast potential this new gaming metaverse holds. In this chapter, we take a magnifying glass to some of those cases, highlighting the shifting landscape of virtual economies and their players.

8.1. Axie Infinity: A Turning Point

Axie Infinity, a blockchain-based game by Sky Mavis, is hailed as the groundbreaker of the Play to Earn movement. The game utilizes creatures called "Axies" that players can train, breed, and engage in battles. These Axies hold real-world value, which can be traded on the Ethereum blockchain.

The game has gained significant attention during the Covid-19 pandemic, specifically in developing countries like the Philippines. Amid job losses and economic downturns, Filipinos found Axie Infinity as a promising alternative source of income.

Jeo, a 22-year-old living in the Philippines, experienced first-hand the power of this movement. After losing his job due to the pandemic, he discovered Axie Infinity. Initially, he saw it as a pastime but quickly realized the earning potential when he started trading Axies on the marketplace. Jeo's monthly earnings now outperform his previous job's salary, allowing him to support his family better during these challenging times.

8.2. Decentraland: Virtual Property Moguls

Decentraland, another blockchain-backed virtual reality platform, provides a different facet of the Play to Earn model. It allows users to create, experience, and monetize content and applications. Here, players can purchase plots of virtual land as Non-Fungible Tokens (NFTs), which can be developed and rented out or sold at a higher price.

Take Sam, for example. A Toronto-based software engineer and keen fan of the concept of metaverse, Sam had bought a virtual land in Decentraland for $500. He spent countless hours developing it into a virtual art gallery, hosting exclusive digital art events. Barely a year later, Sam was offered a staggering $5000 for his digital property. These numbers might seem diminutive compared to real estate figures, but the speed at which virtual land appreciates is nothing short of impressive.

8.3. Cryptokitties: A Collectible Extravaganza

Cryptokitties rose to fame during the late 2017, marking one of the earliest examples of digital collectibles in gaming powered by blockchain. It's a game about collecting and breeding digital cats, and each one holds a unique value. Some rare cryptokitties sold for hundreds of thousands at the peak of their popularity.

Ethan, an ardent gamer from Beijing, started his journey in the world of Cryptokitties purely out of curiosity. However, soon he sold one of his rarest digital kittens for ¥150,000 ($23,000). The astoundingly high price made Ethan realize the earning potential in blockchain games.

While each of these cases bear different elements in the Play to Earn paradigm, the central idea remains constant: gaming time transformed into tangible financial outcomes. These aren't isolated instances; they represent the emergent and open-ended nature of the blockchain-driven gaming sphere. The revolution is here, and it's reshaping the digital world orbit by orbit.

From these stories, one thing becomes clear – the Play to Earn gaming model is not just here to stay; it's set to expand across different types of games, opening up an entire new world of opportunities for players around the globe. Equipped with the fascination of video games and bolstered by the security and transparency of blockchain, this new wave of gaming signifies a seismic shift in the gaming landscape.

As we press forward, curious about the future facets of this gaming metaverse, we must remember the astonishing leaps it's already made, reflected in the successes of Axie Infinity, Decentraland, Cryptokitties, and their countless players worldwide.

Chapter 9. Challenges and Concerns: The Dark Side of Play to Earn

While the advent of 'Play to Earn' gaming promises huge opportunities for gamers around the world, there are several potential challenges and concerns revolving around this emerging ecosystem. In this chapter, we seek to delve into these various issues in an attempt to provide a balanced perspective of the 'Play to Earn' gaming universe.

9.1. Regulatory Risks

One of the primary obstacles facing 'Play to Earn' gaming is the realm of regulatory frameworks. Because these games often involved decentralized finance (DeFi) and blockchain technologies, they fall into a regulatory grey area in many jurisdictions. For instance, the issue of whether in-game assets can be classified as securities under existing financial laws remains unresolved. The ambiguity in the current legal frameworks increases unpredictability for players and game developers, potentially stifearing innovation in the space.

Moreover, widespread establishment of regulatory frameworks could also affect the transferability of in-game assets. Restrictive regulations may limit the capacity of gamers to extract real-world value from their virtual enterprises, thereby undermining the pivotal 'Play to Earn' proposition. Furthermore, it may also impact the cross-game usage of resources and characters, limiting the possibilities of interoperability within the gaming metaverse.

9.2. Securely Storing and Transferring Assets

'Play to Earn' games result in the production of myriad digital assets of significant real-world value. As such, they become potentially attractive targets for hackers and digital thieves. The incidence of hacking and security breaches in the DeFi and cryptocurrency space is not uncommon, presenting a substantial challenge that needs to be addressed.

These games demand robust and secure systems for storing and transferring assets, but achieving such stringent security standards is overbearing for many game developers. Players must trust the underlying technological infrastructure for the safe management, storage, and transfer of their hard-earned assets.

9.3. Economic Inequalities

Another vital issue to consider is the potential for 'Play to Earn' games to foster economic inequalities. Notably, with the increasing acceptance of non-fungible tokens (NFTs) and cryptocurrencies, the initial cost of entering these games can be quite high for many potential players, particularly in developing nations. Additionally, early adopters with substantial resources might create barriers to entry by controlling significant portions of in-game assets and resources, driving asset inflation and making access to the game restrictive for newcomers.

The unequal distribution of assets and wealth within these games could eventually mirror the real-world economic structures and inequalities, contradicting the utopian ideal of an egalitarian digital metaverse.

9.4. Sustainability and Asset Inflation

Investments into in-game assets are based on the assumption that these assets will either preserve or increase their value over time. However, the sustainability of these economic models remains questionable. The value of assets could potentially decrease due to various reasons, like an increase in the supply of assets or a decrease in the game's popularity. Many 'Play to Earn' games rely on the continuous entry of new players, a model that bears a dangerous resemblance to Ponzi schemes.

Capitalization of the gaming economy is another critical concern. Due largely to their novelty, many in-game assets are currently experiencing hyperinflation. A sudden deflation of these inflated asset values could lead to a substantial loss for many players, particularly those who have heavily invested in these assets.

9.5. Mental Health Concerns

'Play to Earn' games have the potential to considerably blur the line between work and leisure. The prospect of earning real-world profits might pressure players to spend extended hours playing these games, leading to gaming addiction and other associated mental health issues. The primacy of profit as a gameplay driver might also cultivate the excessive risk-taking behavior, exacerbating the potential harm to players' mental health.

In conclusion, while the 'Play to Earn' paradigm presents promising potential for the gaming and blockchain industry, it is essential to acknowledge, address and mitigate these associated risks and challenges. Only with a clear and comprehensive understanding of the full landscape can participants - from developers to regulators, and especially gamers - navigate the gaming metaverse with confidence and caution. By tackling these concerns proactively, the industry can undeniably move toward a sustainable, secure, and inclusive future.

Chapter 10. Future Directions: Where is the Gaming Metaverse Headed?

The acceleration of digital technology and creativity is propelling us into uncharted territories, the virtual realms of the gaming metaverse. Each passing day, the frontier extends, inviting us into exciting new possibilities. The once misallocated time sink is now transforming into a potential wealth generator with the employ of blockchain and decentralized finance; however—what does the future hold for the gaming metaverse?

10.1. The Ubiquity of Asset Tokenisation

Asset tokenisation in gaming is currently crafting one of the most intriguing chapters of the metaverse narrative. By using blockchain, digital assets in virtual spaces—land, items, or characters—are tokenised, allowing players to buy, sell, or trade them.

Increasingly, game developers are weaving tokenization into their design matrix, offering users unexampled methods of interaction and creating possibilities for genuine digital property rights. Juxtaposed against the conventional gaming industry, which retains strict ownership norms, asset tokenization democratizes asset ownership, providing players transparent, verifiable, and permanent claims over their in-game items.

Leading these advancements is 'Non-Fungible Tokens' (NFTs). Boasting uniqueness and rarity, NFTs diversify monetary potentialities in gaming, establishing marketplaces where players can trade exceptional assets for real-world value. NFTs reframes the gaming experience, changing 'casual hobbies' into valuable pursuits prospered by tokenized assets. Embedded in this evolution is the prospect for gamers to create unique, valuable digital content that amplifies their economic independence.

10.2. Decentralized Autonomous Organizations (DAOs) and Virtual Governance

Another critical element steering the future course is Decentralized Autonomous Organizations (DAOs). DAOs are opening ambitious avenues for community participation and governance in the gaming metaverse. As DAOs pivot around community-centric models, everyone holds a stake in decision-making processes, ensuring the gaming metaverse's direction aligns with its diverse inhabitants.

Over time, DAOs, a powerful manifestation of decentralized finance, will facilitate the transfer of value within in-game economies, operating as banks, mutual funds, or venture capitalists—a reality bound to attract more participants into the gaming metaverse and lead to its growth and expansion.

Gamers will no longer be just players; they will take on active, administrative roles, contributing to game development and shaping their immersive digital realms. These digital republics promise to give rise to a stimulating era of virtual governance where every player can participate in decision-making symbiotically.

10.3. Proliferation of Digital Real Estate

In a dramatic shift from conventional real estate, the gaming metaverse is ushering in an era of digital real estate—a testament to the incredible potential blockchain technology holds. The ability to own, improve, lease, and trade virtual land creates a vibrant marketplace within the gaming metaverse, one that parallels the real-world property ecosystem.

The future of the gaming metaverse will likely witness an escalation in the value and importance of virtual land. As the virtual world saturates with users, opportunities to develop these lands into productive venues—digital stores, gaming arenas, advertising spaces—become prominent, yielding incredible returns for the investors.

10.4. An Exponential Technological Growth

As the gaming metaverse expands, it will continue pushing against the boundaries of existing technology. Developments in Virtual Reality (VR), Augmented Reality (AR), and High-speed internet, such as 5G, are catalyzing the rise of highly immersive, responsive, and real-time gaming environments.

The metaverse will effectively become a hub for the latest technology, striving to create immersive, flexible, and interactive environments that stimulate our senses just like the real world. Building upon this, as Artifical Intelligence (AI) and machine learning mature further, they will produce more engaging and adaptive in-game ecosystems.

10.5. The Advent of Meta-careers

The future of the gaming metaverse holds out the intriguing possibility of 'Meta-careers'—full-time jobs exclusively nested in virtual environments. Esports players, digital artists, virtual event organizers, architects of digital infrastructures; these are a few examples of the future employment dimension within the gaming metaverse.

As the gaming metaverse's economy stabilizes, the distinction between real and virtual workplaces will blur. The digital expanse is set to become a novel employment landscape, offering jobs that we may have only dreamed of a few years back.

In conclusion, the future of the gaming metaverse is both exciting and unpredictable. With a kaleidoscope of opportunities waiting to be harnessed, and with fluidity and inclusion at its heart, the gaming metaverse is poised to revolutionize the way we play, earn, interact and govern in a digital realm. But this is just the beginning. Where it goes next is a script that's still being written—by every gamer, developer, and innovator daring enough to dream.

Chapter 11. The Novice's Guide: Getting Started in the Play-to-Earn Universe

Welcome, adventurer, as you embark upon a riveting quest through the uncharted terrains of the play-to-earn universe, a cosmos where gaming marries blockchain technology. This virtual realm is an ecosystem where fun meets finance, levity meets liquidity, and entertainment coalesces with entrepreneurship.

While at first glance, this can seem an overwhelming landscape to navigate, fear not! Our comprehensive guide will empower you with knowledge and insights to traverse this new frontier confidently, even if you are a novice in the field.

11.1. The Concept of Play-to-Earn

Play-to-earn, while outwardly a simple concept, has intricate components worth understanding for an effective exploration. In essence, it is an economic model where the gamer receives tangible rewards for their virtual actions or achievements; these rewards can be monetized and offer real-world value.

This approach differs significantly from the traditional gaming model which is essentially 'pay-to-play.' In the conventional format, users purchase in-game assets, expansions or even the game itself. In contrast, the play-to-earn model allows players to earn back, setting up decentralized economies within these digital realms. This paradigm shift is made possible by blockchain technology and decentralized finance (DeFi).

11.2. Understanding Blockchain and DeFi

Blockchain is fundamentally a type of database. Its distinctiveness lies in the way information gets stored; blocks of information are chained together, making modification practically impossible and thus, highly secure. In the realm of gaming, this technology allows for the unique identification of digital items, verifying that they're not replicated or counterfeited.

Decentralized Finance, or DeFi, is a crypto-economic system using blockchain's transparency, security, and rapid settlement features, disintermediating financial transactions. It enables direct peer-to-peer interaction, bypassing the need for conventional financial institutions.

Together, Blockchain and DeFi are creating opportunities for players to own, trade, and profit from their digital assets.

11.3. Choosing the Right Game

As a newcomer, choosing the right game to dive into might seem like a daunting task. Some games offer a low entry barrier, requiring less technical knowledge but potentially fewer in-game opportunities. Alternatively, there are games with higher entry barriers, requiring a deep understanding, but offering more lucrative rewards. Carefully consider your interest level, time commitment, and potential risk before making a choice.

Popular games like Axie Infinity, Decentraland, The Sandbox, and others have already carved a space where players are actively earning. Each conforms to the play-to-earn model but offers different gaming genres. Some are battle games where you control monsters; others allow you to own and monetize virtual land.

11.4. Token Economy and Asset Ownership

Every play-to-earn game has a token economy at its heart. These tokens, which you earn while playing, can be exchanged for other crypto-assets like Ethereum, Binance Coin, or even converted into traditional currency.

Some games have unique forms of tokens — NFTs, or Non-fungible tokens. These digital assets are unique, verifiable with blockchain, and can represent anything from virtual real estate to digital art to in-game characters. Their uniqueness ensures a level of scarcity, giving NFTs potential value within and beyond the game world.

Owning these digital assets means players have real, transferable value derived from their activities within the game. This ownership takes on various forms across different games but essentially means that players can profit through trading, leasing, or utilizing these assets.

11.5. Earning Paths: Trading, Yield Farming, and More

The actual earning within the 'play-to-earn' model can happen through several paths. Trading assets, whether those are NFTs or in-game tokens, based on supply-demand factors, is one way to earn. Astute traders who understand market mechanics can acquire assets cheaply and sell high, thus generating profit.

Yield farming is another method, where players lend their assets for a return. Digital assets staked this way generate yield much similar to how physical property or securities would in the real world.

Furthermore, earning can be as straightforward as receiving rewards for meeting in-game objectives or winning battles, challenges, or competitions.

11.6. Diving into the Deep: Acquiring First Assets

Once you choose a game, the next step — acquiring your first digital assets can be thrilling. Most games require an initial investment, much like the cost of buying traditional video games. Many games offer starter packs that give you a basic set of assets to begin playing. Although these packs are usually not free, considering them as an investment rather than a cost changes the perspective.

As we delve further into the play-to-earn universe, awareness is key. Making informed decisions, understanding risks, and capitalizing on opportunities will become central to your success. And remember, while the goal is to earn, enjoying the game should be a primary focus too. After all, at its heart, play-to-earn is still about experiencing the joy of gaming!

In our subsequent content, we will explore in greater depth the technical aspects of getting started, from creating a digital wallet to mastering key trading strategies. Hold steady, as our expedition into the play-to-earn multiverse continues!

From earning tokens through tutorials to profiting from competitive tournaments, there's a multitude of methods to amass and multiply your virtual wealth. Just remember—as with any investment, patience is critical. It might take time to understand the intricacies, but with perseverance and this guide as your faithful companion, we're confident you can achieve success in this exciting new realm.